CHIEF DAN GEORGE

POET, ACTOR & PUBLIC SPEAKER OF THE TSLEIL-WAUTUTH TRIBE | CANADIAN HISTORY FOR KIDS

True Canadian Heroes – Indigenous People of Canada Edition

www.ProfessorBeaver.ca

Print Edition: 9780228235323
Digital Edition: 9780228235330
Hardcover Edition: 9780228235897

Published by Speedy Publishing Canada Limited

**PROFESSOR
BEAVER**
Building Smarter and Brighter Minds

TABLE OF CONTENTS

QUICK FACTS

Chief Dan George was a famous Tsleil-Waututh Canadian. He was born on July 24, 1899. He was a poet, an actor, a musician, an author, an activist (a person who works for social or political change) and a public speaker. Chief Dan is remembered as a person who helped to educate people about the Indigenous peoples and their cultures. In particular, he taught about the Tsleil-Waututh people.

Did you know?

Indigenous peoples are the first people to have lived in a certain place. There are different groups of Indigenous peoples who live in different parts of Canada. The Tsleil-Waututh are an Indigenous group of people of the Coast Salish which is on the Northwest coast of the Pacific Ocean.

CHIEF DAN GEORGE

CHIEF DAN IS WELL REMEMBERED FOR HIS EFFORTS IN HAVING THE RIGHTS OF INDIGENOUS PEOPLES PROTECTED.

Chief Dan died on September 23, 1981. He is well remembered for his efforts in having the rights of Indigenous peoples protected and having non-Indigenous peoples understand Indigenous culture.

CHIEF DAN'S BIRTH AND EARLY LIFE

Chief Dan was born in the province of British Columbia (B.C.), Canada's most western province. The date of his birth is July 24, 1899 and when he was born, he was given the name Geswanouth Slahoot. He was born on the Burrard Indian Reserve No. 3.

Did you know?

A reserve is an area of land that is for the exclusive (only) use of Indian bands (groups). The bands live on a reserve and their offices are also located there.

VANCOUVER SKYLINE AND BURRARD INLET IN VANCOUVER, B.C.

*Pazifischer
Ozean*

Bull Harbour

*Cape
Scott*

Port Hardy

Winter Harbour

Port
McNeill

*Quatsino
Sound*

Queen Charlotte Strait

Zebulos

Campbell
River

Powell River

*Esperanza
Inlet*

Courtenay

Comox

Nootka

*Nootka
Sound*

Ahousat

*Clayoquot
Sound*

Tofino

Port Alberni

Ucluelet

*Barkley
Sound*

Bamfield

*Vancouver
Island*

Cape
Flattery

Noah B

*Olympic
Peninsula*

Burrard

Anvil I.

Gambier I.

*Howe
Sound*

Bowen I.

*Burrard
Inlet*

Burrard
Inlet 3

VANCOUVER

*Fraser
Delta*

| 0 | 20 km | 40 |

| 0 | 50 km | 100 |

Burrard Indian Reserve No. 3 is an area on an inlet (a piece of land that is shaped liked an arm and is near a body of water). The inlet is located to the southeast of North Vancouver, which is a part of Vancouver, the largest city in B.C.

Chief Dan's ancestry (family members from whom a person descended (came) is the Tsleil-Waututh.

The Tsleil-Waututh live in B.C. and their language is a dialect (variation or type of a language) by the name of Halkomelem. The Tsleil-Waututh used to be called by two different names: the Burrard Indian Band or simply the Burrard Band.

Tsleil-Waututh Nation

PEOPLE OF THE INLET

LOGO OF THE TSLEIL-WAUTUTH NATION

17

ST PAUL'S INDIAN RESIDENTIAL SCHOOL IN NORTH VANCOUVER

Chief Dan spent the earliest years of his childhood living on the reserve. He had eleven siblings. When he was five years old, he was sent to a residential school.

Did you know?

A residential school is a school which Indigenous children were forced to attend. The Indigenous children were taught by non-Indigenous teachers and the language in which they were taught was English. The children were not allowed to speak their first language and they were taught the culture of the non-Indigenous teachers.

Chief Dan started to attend a residential school when he was five years of age. It was at this time that the name that was given to him at birth was changed. At first, it was Dan Slaholt and later it became Dan George.

INSIDE A RESIDENTIAL SCHOOL FOR INDIGENOUS CHILDREN

AS SOON AS CHIEF DAN FINISHED SCHOOL, HE GOT A JOB CUTTING DOWN TREES

It was difficult in the residential school because the students were not allowed to speak their own language or practise their culture. Chief Dan remained in the residential school until he was sixteen years of age. As soon as he finished school, he got a job harvesting trees (or cutting them down and sending them to a sawmill, pulp mill, or a similar facility).

CHIEF DAN'S PERSONAL LIFE

CHIEF DAN AND AMY CECILIA JACK ENTERED INTO AN ARRANGED MARRIAGE.

When Chief Dan was nineteen years old, he got married to a woman by the name of Amy Cecilia Jack. She was Squamish (a group of Salish Indigenous people from the southwest of B.C.) and she was sixteen years of age at the time of the marriage. Chief Dan and Amy entered into an arranged marriage.

Did you know?

An arranged marriage is a marriage that is planned by people other than the people who are being married. Arranged marriages are common in some cultures. Usually, it is the parents or guardians of the married couple who arrange the marriage and agree to the conditions of it.

Chief Dan and his wife, Amy, remained married for fifty-one years. They had ten children, three sons and seven daughters. Two of the children passed away before reaching adulthood. The sons were named Robert, Jesse and Leonard and the daughters were named Amy Marie, Ann, Irene, Rose, Winona, Theresa and Betty.

CHIEF LEONARD GEORGE,
ONE OF CHIEF DAN'S SONS

CHIEF DAN'S JOBS

Throughout his lifetime, Chief Dan had a variety (many different types) of jobs. The different jobs he had were as a stevedore (a person who loads and unloads cargo on to ships), a construction worker, a school bus driver, an itinerant (travels from one place to another) musician, an actor, an author, a poet, a logger and band chief.

CHIEF DAN WORKED AS A SCHOOL BUS DRIVER.

Chief Dan worked as a stevedore for twenty-seven years. From time to time, during the years as a stevedore, he also did some hunting and lumbering. However, in 1947 he had a bad accident in which a large and heavy piece of wood known as timber crashed into him. One of his hips and legs were hurt very badly so he had to retire as a stevedore.

The accident did not stop Chief Dan from continuing to work. He simply changed jobs. As Chief Dan was musically talented, he decided to become an itinerant musician. (Chief Dan played the bass fiddle.) He, along with his children and one of his cousins, formed a group called *Dan George and His Indian Entertainers*. They toured the province of B.C. where they entertained audiences several times a week.

DAN GEORGE AND HIS
INDIAN ENTERTAINERS

Later, Chief Dan George founded (started) a dance group by the name of *Children of Takaya Dance Group*. It focuses on traditional Indigenous entertainment.

CHIEF DAN FOUNDED THE CHILDREN OF TAKAYA DANCE GROUP.

IN ADDITION TO PERFORMING COUNTRY AND WESTERN MUSIC, THE GROUP WOULD PICK HOPS.

The group travelled during the 1940s. Their mode (method) of transportation was a covered truck in which they slept at night. In addition to performing country and western music, they would pick hops. The children were also able to earn money by doing extra activities. It was a very creative way to earn money and Chief Dan considered the time spent doing this as the happiest years of his life.

From 1951 to 1963, Chief Dan was the Band Chief of the Burrard Indian Band, which was later named the Tsleil-Waututh Nation. He also served as the honorary (a job or title given to someone and for which no pay is earned) chief for two other bands: the Sushwap and the Squamish.

NATIVE INDIANS, DRESSED IN FULL REGALIA, PARTICIPATE IN AN ANNUAL SQUAMISH NATION POW WOW.

In the 1960s, Chief Dan became an actor. He starred in a Canadian Broadcasting Corporation (CBC) television series entitled, "Cariboo Country". The way in which Chief Dan came to be selected for his role in the series was very interesting. His oldest son, Robert, was acting in Caribou Country when one of the other actors became too sick to continue.

It so happened that the actor who became sick was playing an Indigenous character. The director (person who is in charge of filming a show) needed to find someone to replace the sick actor as soon as possible. This is when Robert recommended his father, Chief Dan. Although Chief Dan did not have any experience acting, he auditioned (tried out for a role by performing to show one's ability) for the part and got it!

CHIEF DAN STARRED IN A CBC TELEVISION SERIES ENTITLED "CARIBOO COUNTRY" IN THE 1960'S.

Chief Dan turned out to be a very talented actor. After his first acting job, he continued to appear in different roles on television. He also took roles acting in the theatre. He always portrayed (acted as) an Indigenous elder who was kind and gentle. He would never accept a role that portrayed an Indigenous person in a way that was demeaning (actions that make a someone or something lose respect and dignity.

CHIEF DAN STARRED IN THE PLAY "ECSTASY OF RITA JOE" IN 1967.

In addition to acting in Canadian productions, Chief Dan starred in several Hollywood movies. He acted with famous actors such as Dustin Hoffman and Clint Eastwood.

DUSTIN HOFFMAN AND CHIEF DAN IN TH[E] MOVIE "LITTLE BIG MAN" (1970).

CHIEF DAN AND CLINT EASTWOOD IN THE MOVIE "THE OUTLAW JOSEY WALES" (1976).

Chief Dan was also a public speaker and writer who wrote a lot throughout his writing career. In 1967, he gave a powerful speech entitled, "The Lament for Confederation" in Vancouver. It was given during the Canadian Centennial celebrations at the Empire Stadium in front of 35,000 people.

ORIGINAL NEWS CLIPPING WITH FULL TEXT OF CHIEF DAN'S SPEECH

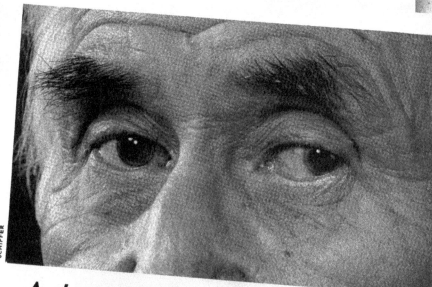

SCHIFFER

A Lament For Confederation

The jubilant crowd of 32,000 at the Centennial Birthday Party in Empire Stadium was silenced by the moving — and bitter soliloquy of Chief Dan George of the Burrard Indian Reserve.

How long have I known you, Oh Canada? A hundred years? Yes, a hundred years. And many many *seelanum* more. And today, when you celebrate your hundred years, oh Canada, I am sad for all the Indian people throughout the land.

For I have known you when your forests were mine; when they gave me my meat and my clothing. I have known you in your streams and rivers where your fish flashed and danced in the sun, where the waters said come, come and eat of my abundance. I have known you ......

I drank your fire-water, I got drunk — very, very drunk. And I forgot.

Oh Canada, how can I celebrate with you this Centennary, this hundred year? Shall I thank you for the reserves that are left to me of my beautiful forests? For the canned fish of my rivers? For the loss of my pride and authority, even among my own people? For the lack of my will to fight back? No! I must forget what's past and gone.

Oh God ...

Did you know?

A centennial is one hundred years and the Canadian Centennial in 1967 was when Canada had become a country for a period of one hundred years.

Chief Dan's speech talked about how poorly the Indigenous peoples were treated in Canada. In the speech, Chief Dan addresses (talks to) the colonialists (those who move to a land, occupy it and control the people who had already been living there).

During the last decade (ten years) that Chief Dan was alive, he became an activist for Indigenous peoples. He worked as a spokesperson whose goal was to educate non-Indigenous Canadians of the culture and traditions of his people.

Chief Dan George: *Actor and Activist*
Le chef Dan George: *acteur et militant*

Longshoreman. Actor. Musician.
Lecturer. Poet. Activist. Environmentalist.
First Nations leader.

Débardeur. Acteur. Musicien.
Orateur. Poète. Militant. Écologiste.
Chef des Premières nations.

CHIEF DAN WAS AN ACTIVIST
FOR INDIGENOUS PEOPLES.

CHIEF DAN'S DEATH AND LEGACY

On September 23rd, 1981, Chief Dan passed away in his sleep at Lions Gate Hospital in North Vancouver, B.C. He was eighty-two years of age. He is buried at Burrard Cemetery in his place of birth.

LIONS GATE HOSPITAL IN NORTH VANCOUVER, B.C., CANADA

CHIEF DAN GEORGE

1899 1981

HIS HEART SOARED LIKE THE EAGLE

GEORGE

In Loving Memory

Our Dad

DANIEL PAUL

CHIEF DAN'S HEADSTONE AT THE BURRARD CEMETERY IN NORTH VANCOUVER, B.C.

Chief Dan has received many honours and awards.

In 1970, he received the New York Film Critics Circle Award and the National Society of Film Critics Award for best supporting actor for his role in "Little Big Man". In 1971, he was nominated for an Academy Award, a Golden Globe Award and a Golden Laurel Award for the same role.

National Society of Film Critics
The Truth, Once Every 12 Months

CHIEF DAN RECEIVED MANY
HONOURS AND AWARDS.

An Academy Award is a famous award that is given to people involved with movies. A Golden Globe Award is a famous award that is given to people for their work in both movies and television. A Golden Laurel Award was given for the same reasons as an Academy Award but, unlike the Academy Awards which holds a grand ceremony, the Golden Laurel Award had no ceremony.

THE OSCAR STATUETTES PRESENTED AT THE ACADEMY AWARDS

When Chief Dan received his nomination, it was the first time that an Indigenous actor had received a nomination for an Academy Award. Although this was a success for Chief Dan, it was also a very sad time. Three weeks before the Academy Awards were presented, his wife, Amy, had passed away.

In 1971, Chief Dan was given the Human Relations Award by the Canadian Council of Christians and Jews.

CHIEF DAN IS PRESENTED WITH A TOTEM POLE BY RICHARD JONES, PRESIDENT OF THE CANADIAN COUNCIL OF CHRISTIANS AND JEWS.

That same year, he was made an officer of the Order of Canada.

CHIEF DAN WAS MADE AN OFFICER OF THE ORDER OF CANADA.

In 1976, Chief Dan was nominated for an Academy Award again for best supporting actor. This time it was for his role as Lone Watie in The Outlaw Josey Wales.

CHIEF DAN AS "LONE WATIE" IN THE MOVIE "THE OUTLAW JOSEY WALES".

In 2008, Chief Dan's image was put on a Canada Post postage stamp.

CHIEF/CHEF DAN
GEORGE
CANADA 52

CHIEF DAN ON A CANADIAN
POSTAGE STAMP

Chief Dan was given an honorary Doctor of Laws Degree from Simon Fraser University (SFU).

CHIEF DAN GEORGE MIDDLE SCHOOL IN ABBOTSFORD, B.C.

Different buildings in Canada have been named in honour of Chief Dan. A school in Toronto, the capital city of Ontario and Abbotsford, B.C. have been called after him. In addition, there is a theatre in Victoria, the capital city of B.C. that has been named in his honour.

Chief Dan's legacy lives on. He is remembered as a very talented man in many different areas. He stood up for the rights of Indigenous peoples and taught the principles of Indigenous culture to non-Indigenous peoples. His lifetime is a testament to the ongoing influence that his works have had on various communities.

He can certainly be considered a true Canadian hero.

CHIEF DAN GEORGE, A
TRUE CANADIAN HERO

Visit

www.truecanadians.ca **TRUE**

to learn about other True Canadian
stories and/or view our catalogue of
edutaining children's books.

CANADIAN SERIES